Increase Brain Power

Improve The Power Of The Brain & Memory Naturally With Proven Methods

Bowe Packer

TABLE OF CONTENTS

PUBLISHERS NOTES

Disclaimer

This publication is intended to provide helpful and informative material. It is not intended to diagnose, treat, cure, or prevent any health problem or condition, nor is intended to replace the advice of a physician.

With that said, please understand that this guide is intended to help get you off to a great start of learning about increasing your brain power. Understand, you will run into things the author did not, that is just the natural process of life.

The author and publisher specifically disclaim all responsibility for any liability, loss or risk, personal or otherwise, which is incurred as a consequence, directly or indirectly, from the use or application of any contents of this book.

Any and all product names referenced within this book are the trademarks of their respective owners. None of these owners have sponsored, authorized, endorsed, or approved this book.

Always read all information provided by the manufacturers' product labels before using their products. The author and publisher are not responsible for claims made by manufacturers.

Paperback Edition 2013

Manufactured in the United States of America

DEDICATION

I dedicate this book to all those people out there who remind us of the things we have forgotten about ourselves.

And this holds especially true of my beautiful and amazing wife, Alma. She is the one woman who has the most amazing talent to let me grow and love the things about myself that I have not fully accepted.

I cherish the love she has for me when I may not know how to love myself.

May we all have this kind of beautiful soul in our life.

Sent from LOVE,

Sunshine In My Soul

HOW TO USE THIS BOOK AND GET THE MOST OUT OF IT

If you want to know how to make your brain work for you better than ever then you're in the right place. This book is written for anyone and everyone that wants to learn how to make themselves smarter and make their mind even stronger. It's also a way that you can better understand how your brain works and what things that you do throughout your life will help it to get stronger. Everything from the way you think to the way you eat will affect your brain and it's time you start doing everything possible in a positive way.

In part one we'll talk about the ways that you can feed your brain to make it stronger and smarter. This section will talk about the great foods that you need to be eating to make a big difference in the way you process information and the way that you think. There's more to it than just eating because you're hungry and it's important that you realize the right things to add to your diet and the ones to take away.

In part two we'll go over a lot of the ways that you can make yourself smarter from activities that you engage in. You'll learn the 'tools of the trade' from mind mapping to journaling. You'll also learn a whole host of other exciting tasks. When you're done with this book and you've put all your new skills into action you'll be smarter and stronger than you ever would have thought possible. So let's get started with the tricks of the trade and the things you need to know to make a difference in your life.

Part I: Starting with the Right Diet To Boost The Power Of The Mind
Introduction

As you get older no doubt you've started noticing more trouble with your memory. It happens to everyone slowly but surely unless they take the initiative and start doing something about it. That's why you've picked up this guide because you really do want to do something about this problem. You're looking to find a way to up your memory so that you don't forget the big important things and also so you don't forget the little things either. I know because I was there once too.

What I noticed was that I wasn't able to remember things like where I put my keys or if I submitted that email to the boss. I also found that I wasn't thinking as fast as I would have liked. It seemed like I was wading through syrup just to get my mind to process what I wanted. I decided it was time to make a change and since you're reading this guide so did you.

I started on my own brain fitness regimen. I knew I had to do something but I wasn't sure about the programs available. I decided that the best thing for me to do was to create my own program. I was going to find a way to strengthen my body in order to increase my brain power. It definitely seemed like a good idea to me and it actually really helped. I was able to remember things better than before and feel better than before as well.

I'm going to share here how I managed to make such a big difference in my life. I'm going to tell you and whoever wants to know all about how I strengthened my brain and improved myself in just a relatively short time. As young people most don't pay attention to the things that their brain needs but the good thing is that you can get most of what you lose back. All it takes is some hard work and you'll be feeling better than ever the natural way.

CHAPTER 1- POWER UP YOUR MIND

Before your brain can really succeed at anything it needs to be nourished. Now nourishment for your mind takes many forms. For one thing you need to be sure that you're getting the mental exercise that you need but you also want to make sure that your body is getting the food that it needs. Without the right food you can't possibly make your brain strong enough to do the things you want it to.

Think about what you normally eat in a day or a typical week. Do you find yourself eating mostly fruits, vegetables and protein? If the answer is yes then you're already a step ahead of the game. If the answer is no however, don't feel too bad, you're actually like a lot of people (and like I used to be as well). Most people at more junk food, sugary drinks like soda and candies. They tend to eat very little fruits and vegetables and that's definitely bad for your body and your brain.

Your brain is very important and it's a very complex organ within your body. In order for those complex actions that it completes (running your entire body) to take place, it needs the right nutrients that it can only get from fruit and veggies. This is the part of your body that controls all of your movements, your thoughts, your emotions and more. That's why it's so important that it receives what it's craving and why it's so important for you to pay attention to what it asks for.

This section is about the food that your body needs and the foods that are best for your brain. These aren't going to necessarily make you super smart but they will definitely help strengthen it. We're not trying to say you need to eat all these foods however but adding the ones that you like best and that fit easiest into your diet will definitely help you in a lot of ways. So start eating these foods and you'll start seeing the difference in your brain process faster than you think.

WILD SALMON

The first thing you need to understand is that wild salmon is *not* the same as the most of the salmon that you purchase in the store. In fact, that salmon is typically raised in a fish farm and has lost most of the great nutrients that a true wild salmon contains. These actually contain protein, amino acids and omega 3 fatty acids which are one of the best products for your body in a lot of ways.

Something else you should know about wild salmon is that it actually helps to prevent cardiovascular disease and Alzheimer's as well. The problem is that salmon grown in fish farms doesn't grow long enough to develop the omega 3 fatty acids that provide these benefits. The wild salmon however, are allowed to grow old enough that they do. So don't settle for the salmon you find in just any store. Seek out the wild ones instead.

CACAO

Yes when we talk about cacao we are sort of referring to those chocolate bars you and everyone else loves to eat. We are not, however, telling you to eat a lot of those bars. The problem with chocolate bars (yes there is a problem with them) is that they are actually full of *processed* cacao that has lost a lot of its health benefits. You can get some of the benefits from chocolate but you won't get as much as you'd like.

What you really want to look for are products made from pure cacao or more pure than regular chocolate bars. You can find chocolate candies that have higher cacao content but just like you'd think they are the darker chocolates. In fact, the darker (and thereby more bitter) the chocolate, the better it is for you. So think about that the next time you start looking for chocolate. You can also find drinks with high levels of cacao.

When you eat dark chocolate you help your brain and also your heart. That's because the dark chocolate has antioxidant rich cacao throughout instead of the small amount used in regular chocolate. In its powder form it can even be added to regular drinks such as coffee for a little extra flavor and a lot of extra healthy benefits as well.

MATCHA

Are you one of the many people that already enjoys drinking tea? Do you drink one or more cups each day? Well if you are then you're already being healthier than others and you're providing your body with some great benefits such as antioxidants. If you drink 4 or more cups each day you can actually increase your lifespan too. However there is an even better type of tea that you probably haven't had before.

Matcha is a powdered tea plant. So instead of a tea bag full of leaves that simply seep the flavor into the water, you actually put the powder into the water itself. So you are drinking the ground up plant itself and therefore receiving all of the benefits that it has to offer.

This plant is used to increase the focus of Buddhist monks who will pray for over ten hours a day. It's also been proven to help with health and even anti-aging. So think about all of these benefits. You could be more focused just that easily by drinking something you may already be drinking each day. If you're not already drinking tea imagine how easy it would be to drink just one or two cups in your entire day? Especially if it's going to improve your abilities so much.

ACAI BERRIES

It's likely that you've heard about the benefits and uses of the acai berry. You may even have tried it yourself or know someone that has. After all, acai berries have become one of the most popular health snacks around. So should you be adding it to your diet? The answer is a definitive *yes*.

Acai berries have a very high level of antioxidants that occur naturally as well as having a high level of protein and yes it is a fruit. These are so great and they're also easy to eat because, as a berry, you can add them to just about anything or simply eat them as a snack by themselves. The important thing however is to get fresh or flash frozen *berries*. Try to avoid pills or powders as these are processed forms that lose much of their health benefits in the process.

BLUEBERRIES

One snack that's always been popular and always been relatively easy to get ahold of as well is the blueberry. These can be found in just about any supermarket and even at roadside markets sometimes. They're also full of great vitamins (a whole variety of them) and they're an easy snack. Of course you'll want to eat more fresh blueberries than blueberries in desserts because when you combine them with sugars you're going to take away from the healthy benefits you get by eating them in the first place.

COFFEE BEANS

No you don't have to eat the coffee beans themselves but what we're suggesting is something you'll probably find quite favorable, drinking coffee. So you don't have to drink tea if you don't like it and can actually continue drinking coffee if you do. Of course it's important to keep a few things in mind about your coffee consumption.

For one thing you want to avoid adding too much sugar and cream into your coffee since this dilutes it (the reason most people do add these things) and also tends to provide you with negative effects. You're also going to want to grind your own coffee beans if you want the best benefits. While pre-ground coffee will provide benefits they aren't quite the same or quite as strong.

If you do drink coffee it's been proven that your risk of Alzheimer's is lessened and the caffeine will help to stimulate your entire body and not just your brain. You probably never knew how much you could really get out of simply drinking something you already enjoy but it's definitely a factor to keep in mind.

WHOLE GRAIN

Whole grains are the ones that actually come up out of the ground and are turned into pastas, breads and other products without the added ingredients. If you generally eat white bread or bleached pasta then you are getting very little actual grain and a whole lot of harmful ingredients. By switching your diet completely you'll get many vitamins and minerals.

Whole grains have the many of the different Vitamin B compounds as well as folate. This means that you'll get improved memory and improved body functions as well. It seems like a pretty good reason to be doing whatever you can.

TOMATOES

Do you eat a lot of tomatoes? Well a lot of people do which is great because tomatoes are so great for you. In fact, they have lycopene which prevents the body from developing dementia. It can also help with a whole host of health effects. This is because of the great variety of vitamins and minerals contained in such as:

- Vitamin K
- Vitamin C
- Vitamin A
- Vitamin E
- Potassium
- Tryptophan
- Copper
- Fiber
- Manganese
- Niacin
- Iron

And still these aren't the only beneficial ingredients in a single tomato. So definitely include it the next time you cook dinner for the family. They'll all thank you for it for the taste and the great health benefits as well.

BLACKCURRANT

Blackcurrants are full of Vitamin C which helps your lungs, immune system *and* your brain. This means it assists in processing memory and sensory input so that your brain works far better every day. It's also a great vitamin in this case because you're getting it from a healthy source.

CHIA SEEDS

Chia seeds are high in omega 3 fatty acids. They're also amazing for your heart and brain. All you need to do is spread them out on bread and you'll be on your way to so much more. This means that you don't have to do much of anything and you'll already be in better shape.

FORTIFIED CHICKEN EGGS

You want fortified eggs rather than the regular because these have more omega 3 fatty acids which help your heart and your brain immensely.

PART II: STRATEGIES FOR BOOSTING YOUR BRAIN AND ITS FUNCTIONING

Are you reading this book to find the one failsafe, quick fix way to increase your intelligence and your thinking ability? If you are then there is one thing you definitely need to know, there isn't one. You're going to need to apply a few different techniques in order to increase your brain power and you're definitely going to need to put some hard work into it. So be prepared that you're not going to get smarter or better brain power overnight.

Part 1 of this book was all about the great foods that you should be adding to your normal diet so that you set your brain up for success. Part 2 is all about the ways that you can use activities and other methods to get your brain working better. So start with the food and then progress from there. You definitely won't be able to succeed without both of these healthy options.

Note: It's important to realize that you won't necessarily succeed quickly and easily at each strategy. Some of them are definitely easier than others and some of them are faster than others at helping your brain. Don't get discouraged and try to accommodate as many of these options into your daily and weekly plans as possible.

CHAPTER 2- MIND MAPPING

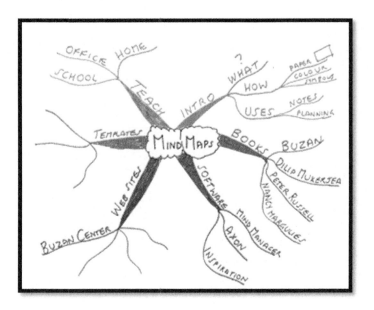

When you were in school did you ever have to make a mind map? A lot of students do but you may not really remember what they are or how they work. That's what we're going to talk to you about. A mind map is a method of creating ideas based around one central idea. Take a look at the image above. That's a mind map and we're going to tell you how to create one for yourself.

What you want is a notepad, dry erase board, chalkboard or sketchpad that's large enough for something like you see above. Don't worry if you need to use more than one piece of paper as long as you remember where all of your lines and notes go. Make sure you also have a method of saving your map if you choose to.

When you look at the map up above it may seem very strange and like it doesn't make a lot of sense. But the truth is that when you create your own map it will make sense. The reason this one doesn't is because you don't know who made it and you don't know what they were thinking about when they did.

Creating a mind map is definitely a very personal experience. That's not to say that you can't share it but you may need to explain your map quite thoroughly to other people whereas you understand it right away. This is because a mind map is literally a map of your thinking process which is completely different from the thinking process of anyone else. So let's get started.

1. The first thing you need is a good idea. This could be your plan to start your own business or your idea for getting an A in your class. Anything you can articulate is a good place to start out. This is what you want to write down in the very center of your paper. You can circle it, underline it or anything you want so that you can have other ideas branch off of it. This first idea

should be quite broad as everything else in your map will branch off. For example you could put 'start a craft store' or 'get an "A" in biology' as your starting point.

2. Next come up with a few things that would help you in your goal and branch those off from the first idea. So if we stuck with 'get an "A" in biology' you could use 'study more' and 'get a tutor.' So you would draw two lines out from your original idea and put one of these on each line. You could have as many items on this level as you want.

3. The third step is to break down each of your last steps even further. You want to eventually get very specific ideas written down that you can put into action immediately. So each time you come up with an idea go ahead and write it down. You don't need to worry if one idea seems to dead end quickly and another has tons of options. That's the point of the exercise is to see what works and what won't.

Chapter 3- Power of Journaling

A journal is a special place where you can keep all of your thoughts, ideas and feelings so that you don't have to keep them all bottled up inside. Some people like to have completely private journals while others use websites to post their journal to friends or even strangers. Whichever type of journaling works best for you it's important to give it a try for several reasons.

1. People who journal have less stress

2. Journaling is a way to organize thoughts and ideas
3. Journals give you someone to 'talk to' about problems you may be facing
4. Journals can provide an outlet for anger or other emotions

Your options for journaling are numerous. You can use any notebook or sketchpad you like. You could buy a special journal or decorate your journal in some way. Some people like to have a journal with a lock and key so others can't read it. Others may like to create a file on their computer that they can save their information to or create a blog so others can read what they write. The choices are endless and all you need to do is find the one that works best for you.

One of the biggest questions that people ask when it comes to journaling is 'what should I write?' Well that's actually the beauty of it. You should write whatever you want. Anything that comes to your mind can be put into that journal and it should too. Don't worry about writing slowly and neatly, no one really needs to be able to read your journal after your write it. Don't worry about spelling and grammar and all of that or even about making sense. Just write down what you're thinking, feeling or even dreaming about.

The point of journaling is to get all of your thoughts and ideas out there. This can help when you're feeling strongly about something or when you're having a fight with someone you care about. It can also help when you're trying to start a new project and you don't know where to go or you're trying to write a story and you want to get your notes out before you forget them. Don't be afraid to write anything and everything.

Now make sure that you're enjoying your journaling when you do it because if you don't you'll be taking away from the exercise. If you enjoy journaling you'll write more and you'll achieve more from it. If journaling is a chore to you then you'll simply be annoyed to have to scrape out a paragraph or two each day. Only journal when you feel like it. You may only get a few sentences one day and five pages the next. That's okay and actually it's exactly what you need to get your mind going.

CHAPTER 4- POWER NAPS

Yes I said nap. Well right there you're probably excited for this one aren't you? Well power naps are actually known to help your body to recover and help your brain to feel refreshed and stronger. If you're one of those people that only gets 4 or 5 hours of sleep a night then you definitely need this. If you're getting the proper 8 to 10 hours you could still use it. That's because sleeping more can actually help your body in many ways.

Not getting enough sleep increases your risk of cancer, stroke, heart attack and more. It can also decrease your brain power and cause you to get sick more often. By getting the right amount of sleep you can lessen your chances for all of these. Just make sure that your naps aren't taking too long or you could actually end up having even more problems with being tired all the time.

A 15 to 30 minute nap in the middle of the day is the best thing for you. This allows your body to relax and recharge for the rest of the day. Your brain gets the opportunity to chill out and that means when you wake up again it's ready to start thinking about new things and getting the things you need done. By reducing your fatigue and the workload on your brain you can speed up the way that it things and operates.

CHAPTER 5- LOWER YOUR BLOOD PRESSURE

Having low blood pressure is a good thing for people of all ages but especially as you start getting older. This is because high blood pressure causes a whole host of disorders and diseases including decreased brain function. If you have trouble with your memory and your thought processes and you have high blood pressure chances are that this one simple step will do wonders for you.

Lowering your blood pressure is something you need to talk with your doctor about. They will know the best options for you and for your specific bodily needs. They may recommend some diet changes or even medications. Think about how much these changes will do for you in the long run and definitely do whatever you can to make them. You'll be glad you did.

CHAPTER 6- MEDITATE

Meditation is excellent for your body and your brain in more ways than we can even hope to describe here. So we're going to just stick with the biggest reasons that adding meditation to your life will make big changes and definitely for the better. It doesn't matter if you're religious, spiritual or anything else because you don't need to have any specific beliefs. All you need is a willingness to try new things and an ability to relax and empty your mind.

By practicing meditation you'll be able to lower your anxiety and calm your nerves. You'll also be able to improve your breathing and lower your blood pressure. All of these together will help you to decrease the amount of stress you experience as well as any pain that you may experience.

When you're having trouble concentrating on something or you're having difficulty figuring out the solution to a problem just take a moment to sit back and relax. Meditating can help you to solve your problems as long as you know the proper way to do it and you give it a try. So let's go through what you need here.

The first thing you need is to find a comfortable place and way to sit. You can stand or lay down if you want but remember the goal is relaxation. You don't want to be stiff and you don't want to fall asleep either. You also want to be somewhere quiet where you won't be interrupted. If you relax better with music then put it on softly in the background.

Close your eyes and concentrate on your breathing. Try to empty your mind of all thoughts and only breathe in silence for a few minutes. You could meditate for only two or three minutes or for a half hour if you choose. You could also choose to set aside time for meditation each day or simply engage in it whenever you have a spare moment or need to relax. There's never a right or wrong time or place.

If you want to learn even more then don't be afraid to search online or pick up a book. There are plenty of different places to learn all about meditation and plenty of reasons to do it as well. You'll find yourself more refreshed after meditation then you do after a nap and your brain will get stronger every time.

CHAPTER 7- GET FIT FOR LIFE

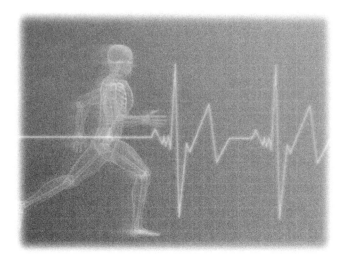

When you exercise you aren't only improving your muscle and joints. You're also improving your brain. Think about how you exercise and what happens to your body when you do. Do you really think that your mind doesn't have anything to do with it? Well if you do then you would definitely be wrong. The brain has so much to do with your physical exercise.

Some people like to give in to their food cravings and think this is helping their mind. They think because their brain is telling them to eat those things they must be helping but that's not the case. Those things also won't help you with your thought process and will actually slow you down.

So how do you use fitness to improve your brain? Well actually any type of physical fitness will help and you don't even have to go to a gym to do it. You're also not going to have to become a bodybuilder and lift a lot of weights. Instead, you can find a fun activity that also requires you to get a little bit of exercise like one of these:

- Martial arts
- Kickboxing
- Walking
- Jogging
- Dancing
- Swimming
- Karate
- Rollerblading
- Skiing
- Aerobics
- Surfing

Of course these are only a few of the different exercises you could try and I'm sure you can find plenty more if you just look online or look up the classes offered in your neighborhood. You'd probably be surprised at all the things that are offered very reasonably and that you'll actually enjoy. Each time you engage in one of these you'll also improve your brain as well as your entire body.

Chapter 8- Exercise with Games

Sitting around and doing nothing will actually decrease your brain power as well. So make sure that you're always up and moving around and doing something you enjoy. One of the big things you should be doing is playing games of all types. Whether it's video games, board games, word games or puzzles make sure you're engaging your mind and giving it the stimuli that it needs to be strong. You've probably heard the phrase 'use it or lose it' and it definitely applies to your brain.

Don't think about games as being 'only for children' because you'll miss out on a lot of fun. Not only are there plenty of adult games available, the children's ones can be fun too. Board games or card games allow you to have fun with someone else (your spouse, friend, or children) and also help to get your mind going.

Of course there are plenty of more technological options as well. For one thing you can play games on your computer, smartphone or tablet. You can also use any type of gaming console. Chances are that you have at least one and possibly several of these options which can be played by yourself or with someone else. Even better you get to choose the types of games you like to play which vary from word puzzles to action and adventure games.

Of course it's important to remember not to get carried away with your video games and to make sure that you're not playing too much. A few hours a day is fine but any more than that and you could actually be harming your brain more than helping.

CHAPTER 9- CURL UP WITH A GOOD BOOK

Do you enjoy reading? Well if you don't then you should start looking for some good books that you will enjoy reading. That's because books are excellent for your brain and also for your stress level. When you read you're able to escape to another place and into a world that you love. It's like getting away from your life for a little while which exercises your brain and helps you feel more relaxed when you're done.

You don't need to have a hard copy book with actual paper pages anymore. You can read from your tablet, smartphone or computer which makes it easy to take an entire library with you no matter where you go or how much space you have.

When you read it can expand your mind. Whether you read fiction or non-fiction your brain has to process everything that you're reading. Your brain thinks about those things later on too as it tries to process and remember the things its read. Good writers can make you really feel like you're in the action so your brain tries to help you hear, smell and even taste the things that you're reading thus exercising it even more.

Take a few minutes to stop by your local library or even an online book site and pick out something. Just give it a try for a few minutes a day. You can find books that are completely free. No matter where you get the books or what type you choose to read you'll be happy that you gave it a try once you start reading. You'll be having more fun and you'll also be getting better brain power while you're at it.

CHAPTER 10- DO SOMETHING DIFFERENT

Have you been doing the same old thing every day for the past ten years? If you are then you're like a lot of people but you're not doing anything for your brain. Your brain needs new adventures and opportunities in order to advance. It needs to have new experiences and try new things in order to be stronger. So don't get stuck in a rut.

- Build a model plane, train or car
- Learn a new language

- Learn to play a musical instrument
- Volunteer at a homeless shelter or library
- Learn to write with your non-dominate hand

Learning something new will make your brain work harder as it struggles to not only hear and understand the instructions you're giving it but also to remember them. Later when you actually start using your new skills it will have to remember those things that it was taught and apply them in the correct situation. It's a great way to have some more fun in your life as well as strengthening your brain because you'll be getting to experience something completely new.

CHAPTER 11- SPEND TIME WITH PEOPLE

Did you know that socializing can improve your mental ability? Well if you think about some of the conversations that you have with your family and friends you may not be as surprised. That's because socialization will cause you to think and it will also help you to relax and prepare for the other things you'll need to do throughout the days, weeks and years of your life.

Spending time with people is actually a necessity for a happy and healthy life so definitely don't take it for granted. You'll have a lower risk of depression and also a lower risk of mental illness if you spend a decent amount of time with other people on a regular basis.

Of course how you socialize is entirely up to you. You may prefer having a few friends over for a quiet movie night or a nice dinner or you may like to go out on the town and visit a bar or club. The way you do it is entirely up to you as long as you're with other people and you're not engaging in stressful situations.

CHAPTER 12- USE YOUR IMAGINATION

You may think you're too old to be daydreaming about faeries and castles and being a knight but the truth is that you're not. In fact, daydreaming about things that don't exist or even things that do in a way that you wish they would turn out is an excellent exercise for your brain. It's a perfect way to expand your thought process and leave yourself open to new ideas at all times.

If you're not sure how to get started then just start with observation. When you first wake up sit up in bed (or you could stay lying down if you're more comfortable) and think about how you're feeling. Think about your dreams from the night before and the way you feel right now. Think about what you see or smell. What do you think about the way the light shines in through the window or your cat winds its way through the shadows?

Whenever you have a moment just take some time to really look around and see the things around you. Whether you're at work, on the subway or eating lunch just look at what's happening. What about that couple that's talking quietly by the door? Are they up to something? Maybe they're spies about to engage on a top secret mission or maybe they're lovers hiding from a jealous husband. They could be anything you want them to be.

If you take some time to think about people and places and events in new ways you'll find your imagination working overtime before you know it. Just a simple smell could trigger you to think of something strange and exotic or maybe you see someone in a certain color that makes you think of a story you once read. Take the time to let your mind overwhelm you with stories and ideas.

Thinking about things in a new way can also help you to be more imaginative. Think about the man with a 'dapper smile' instead of just a nice smile or the woman with the 'effervescent glow.' Thinking about something in a different way or a more imaginative way can really help you to see the beauty and the imagery in everything around you.

Next time you tell a story try to engage the other person so they really feel like they were there. Tell them about the things you heard and smelled and saw. Don't just tell them what happened; paint a picture so they actually feel like they were right there with you.

If you want to use this as part of your journaling then go right ahead. You may find yourself creating interesting stories out of thin air simply by listening and absorbing the things around you.

Chapter 13- Change it Up and Make it Exciting

You've probably heard the phrase 'don't rock the boat.' Well in this section we're going to tell you that you definitely *do* want to rock the boat because that's what's going to get your mind going again and help your brain to feel more stimulated. The same old thing over and over again gets boring and after a while your brain doesn't need to do anything to complete those tasks so it simply gets them done. As a result you feel upset. So change things up.

- Redesign-Take a look around your house and think about the ways that you can make it even better. You can actually have a lot of fun with this and step out of your comfort zone at the same time. Try to think of ways that you can make the rooms in your house even better whether its design-wise or simply moving around furniture to make the house more 'user friendly.'

- Redecorate-Make your space more interesting by adding some new knickknacks or even artwork. You could even use new throw pillows or ornamental plants to make the space look different. You'll be helping yourself to feel better at the same time by exploring your imagination and what you think would work best in your home.

Chapter 14- Use All Your Senses

Do you find yourself experiencing life through your sense of sight? A lot of people do this and it's great for seeing what's around you but it's not the only way to experience things. Typically, it's also not the way that people really experience either. That's because chances are there are a lot of things that happen around you that you don't actually see because they simply aren't interesting enough or you subconsciously don't deem them important enough to really look at and understand.

This section is about using your sense of sight to its best ability but also about using all of your other senses. If you're like a lot of people you don't really take the time to experience things through your sense of taste or smell. You may not really think about listening to what happens around your or touching things to experience them. So take a moment to really think about these other senses.

1. Smell- Next time you walk into any place whether it's the mall or a flower shop take a moment to smell what's around you. Think about the different flowers or people that are around you. What do you smell and what can you tell about them based on that smell? Can you pick out different people or different flowers?

In the mall you may be able to pick out different groups of people such as older or younger individuals. You may also be able to pick out different stores based on the smell or different restaurants. In a flower shop you may be able to pick out the flowers that are present in the area. Don't use your eyes, use your nose.

2. Hearing-Take a moment to hear what's happening around your house. Sit on the porch and simply open your ears to what is happening. Can you hear the kids playing in the yard next door? How about your neighbor leaving for work or the people next door who are discussing their car problems. You can imagine the things that are happening around you without actually seeing them. All you need to do is listen and you'll be right in the thick of things.

3. Touch-You don't even need to leave your own home to practice using your sense of touch. Walk around the different rooms of your house and try touching different things. Feel the tablecloth in your dining room and the curtains in the living room. What about the bedspread in your room or the clothes in your closet? Chances are there are a variety of different fabrics throughout your house.

Take a moment to close your eyes and experience the feel of those fabrics as you touch them. You could simply touch them with your hand or rub them against your face. Think about what it is based on how it feels against your skin.

4. Taste- When you taste something you usually only think about whether it's good or bad. You think about whether you really like it or not. You may taste it enough to think about whether or not it's sweet, sour, hot, cold or spicy. What you probably don't do is think about all the individual ingredients in that food.

Next time you eat a meal whether you've made it yourself or you're eating out take a moment to try to pick out the different flavors and ingredients in the dish. You may think you're no food connoisseur but you'd be surprised how many ingredients you can actually pick out based only on the taste of the food in your mouth.

Try not to actually look at the bite before you eat it. You may see something on the food that gives away an ingredient but if you simply take that bite you'll have to experience what's there by what you can taste. If you move the bite around in your mouth you'll taste more aspects of the food and you'll be able to pick out even more.

5. Sight-All right so now we come to the sense that you probably use most of all, your sight. So what do you really see in a day? Do you really see everything that happens around you? Chances are that you don't because hardly anyone actually does. What you want to do is train your eyes to see more than just what's directly in front of you.

When you go somewhere try to look around and see everything that's happening. Look at every person and every object. You don't need to move from one spot to get a really good look at what's happening around you and truly understand it.

Take some time to write down your experiences in your journal. By using each of your senses you get a better experience of the world around you. The different areas of your brain also get a good workout because of the different senses you employ. You'll also never make the mistake of only using one sense for something again.

CHAPTER 15- LEARN TO LOVE THE MUSIC

Music has been around much longer than you or I or anyone we've ever known. In some form or another it's been played likely since the beginning of humans on the planet. There are different styles that appeal to different people and different volumes that you can play it at but just about everyone loves some form of music or another. What we want to talk about is how you can increase your brain power through music.

For one thing music can actually calm people down. You may be surprised to learn that some people are calmed by rock music or even rap while others need classical music to calm down. Any type of music can help you to feel better when you're stressed or overly anxious about something. Just realize that you will feel stressed in life and if simply listening to a good song could make you feel better wouldn't you want to give it a try?

Besides just lowering your stress level, music can actually lower your blood pressure as well. It also helps to lessen the effect of dementia and increase weight gain in those who are underweight. Preemie infants have seen these benefits help them to grow stronger faster. You'll see them as you feel stronger in all aspects of your life and not just in your brain.

Playing music can help your brain even more. This is because your corpus callosum (the section of the brain that links the two sides) is improved by listening to and playing music. By learning how to play an instrument you can also increase your motor cortex which will help you with a number of other tasks that you likely complete quite regularly.

Finally, playing music will help your spatial skills. Your brain works to learn better and better as you continue to play which means you don't need to worry too much about being bad. You'll quickly learn to be good which improves your brain as well.

Find a musical instrument that you've always liked whether it's the harmonica, the saxophone or a set of drums. There are thousands of instruments around the world that you could pick up and there's a teacher out there somewhere or a book available that will help you to learn. You'll be showing off to your friends in no time at all.

CHAPTER 16- BREATHE IT OUT

Nearly everyone has heard of Buddha (born Siddhartha Gautama). Most know him because of his ability to meditate for extensive periods but many don't know how he went about doing just that. Well we're going to tell you the secret, breathing. Yep, that's it. Breathing.

By breathing the right way you can help yourself to relax and calm down. When combined with the meditation we talked about earlier these methods of breathing can help you immensely by getting rid of stress and fatigue and even helping to improve your ability to concentrate for long periods of time. All it takes is the right technique and you'll be able to do it all the time.

What you want to do is learn to breathe deeply and rhythmically. You don't want to take short, quick breaths because these don't provide the amount of oxygen to your brain that is needed. What you need is a deep breathe which fills your lungs and expels all the carbon dioxide in your body. So you need to learn how to breathe this way. Once you do, you'll never go back to your old way of breathing again.

By breathing from your chest like most people do you actually hurt your chest muscles and increase the fatigue you feel. That's because breathing from your chest doesn't provide enough oxygen and when your brain doesn't get enough oxygen you start to feel tired. (That's also why you yawn in case you didn't know, so that your brain can get more oxygen.) So how do you practice proper breathing?

1. Find a comfortable place to sit whether it's on your bed, couch or a chair. You can even sit on the floor if you're most comfortable there. Make sure that you're in a quiet place that's not too bright.

2. Make sure you're sitting up straight but not forcing your back too straight where it's uncomfortable. You want to be slightly relaxed.

3. Keep your head upward so that your neck is straight and your eyes are facing forward. You should be looking at the wall straight ahead of you. Again make sure that your neck is straight but still lose enough that you don't get stiff.

4. Take a deep breath imagine that your stomach is a balloon you're trying to fill. Your stomach should

expand outward as you inhale and your chest should puff up slightly. You want to take in as much oxygen as you can with that deep breathe but remember that it should come in through your nose and not through your mouth.

5. When you exhale you want to let the air out through your nose as well. You should feel your stomach deflate and your chest sink back down.

6. If you want to meditate you can add this in to your breathing exercises. It's much easier than you might think because you simply sit just like you already are, close your eyes and breathe like we said.

7. Meditating for about five minutes is a great place to start. You may want to just go for as long as you feel like the first few times or you may want to set an alarm to bring you back. Make sure it's not too sharp or you'll break the stress less feeling you've just created by meditating and breathing properly.

CHAPTER 17- NUTRITIONAL SUPPLEMENTS THAT WORK

There are literally thousands of different nutrition supplements available on the market. These range from your normal vitamins and minerals to different plants, herbs and mixtures that are meant to help you do everything from eat less to see better. You'll find something (and likely a lot of something's) for anything you want or need.

In this book we're not going to focus a lot on the different supplements available since you can find that information just about anywhere you look. If you want a lot of information check online for the problem you're suffering from or the type of supplement you're thinking about taking. You'll find information about what to do, what the supplements do and all the different options you have.

If you're looking to increase your brain abilities however there are two supplements that you should be looking at primarily. These are gingko biloba and St. John's wort.

Gingko biloba seems to be a cure for quite a lot of things. At least if you ask people around the world they seem to think so. It's been said to cure just about any condition you could have including problems with concentration and thinking. All you have to do is mix it into your tea or find a tea that's made with this product and you'll be able to start reaping the great benefits. It's also available in other forms and from a variety of different companies. So find one that works best for you.

This is also a very inexpensive supplement because it's easy to grow and easy to find. It's also very simple to take because you don't need very much of it for the great results. It will help to increase blood flow to your brain with just 1 or 2 tablets each day. How easy is that to take?

St. John's wort is a slightly less well known supplement that hasn't been around for quite as long. In fact it's only been around for about 10 years now though it has excellent reviews for its uses. The most important use (for us anyway) of this supplement is its ability to make you happier the natural way.

St. John's wort can help you feel less upset and depressed though no one is quite sure why. It's important however that you talk with a doctor if you're having very depressive thoughts and definitely before taking either of these or any other supplement. Not everyone can take supplements without side effects.

Even though most supplements are made of natural ingredients not all of the ingredients are always natural. Not only that but sometimes supplements can contain ingredients (even all natural ingredients) that an individual is allergic to or that could cause side effects when combined with medications.

CHAPTER 18- THINK, THINK AND THINK SOME MORE

Do you think about things frequently? Do you feel like you think as much as the people around you or do you feel like you spend less of your time thinking than others? What about the way that you solve your problems and create your plans throughout life? Even little things like what to eat for lunch or when to water the flowers are decisions that you should take a moment to think about. More important decisions require even more thought and consideration.

What you want to do is think more often. When you have a problem or are approached with an idea don't instantly act on it. Many people feel that they should react quickly and follow their instincts but this is not always the best choice to make. You want to make sure that you are taking time to really weigh out the options and make a decision after you have done this. You'll feel less anxious if you weigh out your choices.

What you want is called critical thinking. It's a method of problem solving where you think about the problem and discover the best way to solve it. One of the best ways to do this is with the mind mapping task we talked about earlier in this book. Write down the problem in the center and some very basic ways to solve it branching out. As you continue you'll find new and inventive ways to solve the problem or reach a new solution.

No matter what type of problem you're facing you can solve it through thinking it out. Sure you may have to do a little research if, for example, you're looking into buying a new roof and don't know if you want shingles or aluminum. You may want to ask opinions from people around you or from experts. You'll also want to get quotes on the price and how long the job will last. All of these things can go on your mind map. So the center would be 'new roof.' The next ring could be all the considerations you have such as 'length of use,' 'initial cost,' 'upkeep cost,' etc. Then you could come up with the different options from there.

1. Step one is to write out your problems or worries as they come to you. Never ignore something that you're concerned about because it will only continue to fester and continue to worry you as time goes on.

2. Find out all the relevant information about your problem and write it down with the problem itself. If you don't understand the problem then get help from someone else or from a reputable source. Make sure

you thoroughly understand all aspects of the problem before moving on.

3. Take a moment to think about the following questions:

    a. What would solving this problem do for you?
    b. What's the worst case scenario if you can't solve this problem?
    c. What do you need to do to overcome the problem?

4. Now that you've answered all of these question's you actually know what you can expect if things don't go the way that you want them to. You know what you're going to do if you can't solve the problem and you even know what will happen if you do.

5. Next you want to figure out solutions to the problem. Think of absolutely everything that would make the problem better no matter how farfetched it may seem. Try to get at least ten options that you can go over and choose from.

6. Figure out the most reasonable solution. Which option that you've come up with seems like it's the best choice? Give it a try. If it works then you're already done. If it doesn't then you've still got a whole list of other options that you can try out. Don't get discouraged and if you run out of options simply try to come up with some more.

CHAPTER 19- GIVE HYPNOSIS A TRY

If you've never tried hypnosis then this is a way that you can start without all the embarrassing stuff like spilling your guts in front of strangers. All you need is a recording that you can play on your phone, computer, radio or tablet. Then you can play it anytime you need a little help.

Hypnosis helps you to relax and also helps you to increase your concentration. It's great for a number of reasons actually including the ability to improve your creativity and your methods of expressing yourself, becoming more organized and increasing your confidence.

When you use hypnosis you're not using 'black magic' and you're not going to get hurt either. What you're doing is bringing out a different part of your mind, the subconscious, to help you make helpful changes in your life. This helps you to use your mind to work for you. You will be stronger and smarter before you know it with this method.

The hypnosis that you use this way is a script that gives you suggestions for your future and your life. You aren't required to follow those suggestions and you won't be forced to either.

Bowe Packer

This isn't like the hypnosis that you see in movies or on TV where you're completely out of control. You'll still have control but you'll be able to bring out your subconscious mind and thoughts as well.

In case you're worried still hypnosis is actually approved by the FDA and it's considered a true method of therapy. You'll be able to help yourself and won't need to worry so much about what you've seen in the movies.

CHAPTER 20- BECOME A SPEED READER

No we're not learning about a way that you can quickly learn to read. What we're talking about is speed reading. Being able to skim through a page quickly enough that you don't spend a lot of time but you still get the gist of the material. This is a great thing for someone who wants to improve brain functioning because reading quickly and still retaining the information you read requires a lot of skill and a high level of brain function.

CHAPTER 21- YOUR SUBCONSCIOUS WORKS FOR YOU

Your brain has two different parts that work together for you to get through your day and your life. These are the conscious and subconscious parts of the brain. One (the conscious) does the things you think about doing such as saying things or studying while the subconscious takes care of things like breathing and making your heart beat.

What you may not know is that your subconscious is also where your imagination is and it's where most of your deepest thoughts and dreams are stored. As you get older this part of your brain typically isn't used as much as you start to grow up and daydream less often. But what you want to do is help your subconscious to continue working well so that you are embracing your childlike side.

When you get rid of your subconscious mind you are actually stifling your own creativity. You are keeping yourself from being as inquisitive as you'd really like to be and are also keeping yourself from being a more fun and adventurous person.

Think of your subconscious as your friend. Make them someone that is different from you and has their own way of speaking. Then carry on a conversation with yourself. Think about the things your subconscious wants to think about for a change. You might learn something new and you'll be exercising the more fun part of your brain while you're at it.

CHAPTER 22- BUILD A PUZZLE

A puzzle doesn't have to be 1000 pieces and take you three weeks to finish. In fact, puzzles can be very small or they may not involve pieces at all. Word puzzles or Sudoku for example are types of puzzles that don't use pieces. Pick a type of puzzle that you enjoy and have fun trying to solve it. Any type of puzzle will exercise your mind in different ways and help it to become stronger.

When you have some free time sit down and pick up a puzzle. Decide which type or types are your favorite and try to devote at least 15 minutes a day to solving a puzzle. You may not finish one every day and some days you may finish five but just taking the time out of your free time will help you to make the most out of every moment of the day.

If you like puzzle books then pick one up at your local dollar store and play while you're waiting for the bus or even while you're riding the bus to work. Or you could download one on your tablet, computer or smartphone that you can play no matter where you are without having to remember your puzzle book every day.

Spending just a few minutes a day on puzzles will help you in many ways and the longer you spend the more you'll do for yourself.

Chapter 23- Get To Know Yourself Better than Anyone

Do you really know yourself? You probably think that you do but what do you really know? Think about the things that you really like and really don't like and try to figure out why. Chances are you may not have ever thought about it before but those things are very important to who you are.

When you don't understand yourself you tend to trip up on emotional baggage and problems. By understanding yourself better you're able to actually solve your problems and feel better about yourself. You're also able to change things that you may not like or understand about yourself without worrying about what others will think.

CHAPTER 24- BE YOUR OWN MOTIVATION

What you may have noticed throughout your life is that your brain tends to respond quite often with the phrase 'I can't.' Whether you're talking about climbing the monkey bars or becoming partner in a law firm your brain almost seems hardwired to make you fail and what happens? You fail. That's because you don't believe in yourself.

When your mind thinks things that's what it works towards. This is because your brain actually doesn't have a clue what the difference between imagination and real life is. When you think about something enough it starts to believe it's true and works harder to reach that goal and that reality. So make sure that you're using positive affirmations to make the things you want come true.

A positive affirmation is a positive statement such as:

- 'I will lower my blood pressure.'
- 'I will solve my own problems.'
- 'I will lose 100 pounds.'
- 'I am the best at what I do.'
- 'I am the best worker here.'
- 'I will write a bestselling novel.'

Try coming up with at least five positive affirmations for yourself every day. You may decide you're going to come up with your affirmations each morning before you get up or sometime during the day when you feel depressed or upset. If you come up with five that you feel strongly about you could choose to simply repeat them to yourself every morning or whenever you're feeling upset.

Positive affirmations help you to reach your goals and do the things you want to do in life. Use your imagination to your advantage and make yourself stronger than you ever were before.

CHAPTER 25- DECREASE STRESS, INCREASE YOUR POWER

The stress response in your body is a way of reacting to potential danger. Your body starts preparing for something bad to happen and then reacts in the best way it knows how. When you start feeling stressed your body is telling you to do something now before problems come up.

In ancient times stress would go away quickly as the reason for the stress went away as well. In more modern times however it seems that stress is more difficult to get rid of. This is because the reasons for your stress are a little more complicated now and a lot more difficult to get rid of. Society has grown and having a stress free life has continued to become more and more complicated as time has gone on. That's why it's important to really think about the things you're doing in your life because stress decreases your brain power.

As your body continues to build up stress it starts to break down. This is when you start to feel upset and you also start to feel sick. Often your mental abilities start to wear down until you feel like you just can't think anymore. If you don't deal with the stress you feel this continues to get worse and worse as time goes on. After years of these problems you actually can cause permanent problems for your brain.

Stress management becomes very important when you start experiencing these problems because without it you could continue to have more problems until you are unable to function throughout your normal life because of the difficulty you're experiencing.

Stress can actually kill you because of its tendency to cause high blood pressure and cardiovascular disease. For these reasons (and for the many more disorders high stress can cause) it's important to put these tips into action:

1. Take control of the situation. Wherever you are when you feel stressed try to gain control of the things around you. It may be that you don't have the ability to change things such as the way the office is run or the way that your husband drives the car but you may be able to change some situations you are in that you don't care for.

If you find yourself in a situation that causes you stress try to do whatever you can to get out of the situation or change it so that you don't experience the same stress. Even if you can lessen the amount of stress you feel it will be a benefit to you. You'll also want to talk to others if you feel that you can't change the situation but someone else can.

Be willing to stand up for yourself and the things you think are right. You don't want to feel stressed all the time and you don't deserve to either. That means you need to take the initiative to change things or talk with others about changing things. By talking about the problems you are having you can work out good solutions with others.

2. Make your goals reasonable. If you set a goal to change the world you have a very low chance of actually succeeding at it. You don't want to spend your entire life reaching out towards a goal that you have a high likelihood of failure on. You may choose to set a goal like this one but only if you have a plan for how to achieve it and you set smaller goals along the way.

When you accomplish a goal it helps you to relieve some of the stress you experience as you reach towards the goal. For example if you set a goal to lose 20 pounds this year you'll likely feel some stress as you work towards the goal but when you reach that 20 pound mark you'll feel much more relaxed and you'll relieve the stress.

3. Avoid the stress. If you're experiencing a situation that causes you to feel stress then take a few moments and get away from it. Stress has a cause of some type even if you can't figure it out right away. Take a few minutes to think about when you're feeling stressed and why. Next you'll want to try and get away from that stressful thing as quickly as you can.

Getting away from something that causes you stress is much easier than you may think. Even if you are having a fight with someone and that's your stressor you can get away for a short time. When you've had a few moments to collect yourself and relax you can come back to the person. Getting away from the stress doesn't mean you have to avoid it forever. It just means taking a break.

4. Don't expect perfection. You're not a perfect person. Much as you may like to be (and I would like to be as well) no one is perfect. You can't expect yourself to be because when you expect nothing but perfection from yourself you actually cause more harm than good. You're likely to increase your mental anguish and your stress and cause yourself to burnout.

Think about all the things you're trying to accomplish and try to reconsider. Do you really need to do all 23 things on your to-do list or can you cut it down to 10? Do you really need to attend every bake sale at your child's school as well as every field trip, all your work trips and every one of your wife's big meetings? Chances are that you don't need to do all of those things.

Try to come up with the most important things that you absolutely need to do or that you absolutely want to do. Shave a few off the top of your to-do list and you'll start feeling much better about yourself because you'll be less stressed.

If this doesn't work for you then try creating a list. The first list is all the things that absolutely have to be done right away. These are things like paying your taxes and paying the mortgage. Things on the second list are ones that need to be done soon such as paying the car insurance at the end of the month or going grocery shopping. Finally, the third list is things that you want to do but don't necessarily *need* to do such as those school field trips with your child.

CHAPTER 26- CRAVE SOMETHING NEW

When you get bored with your surroundings you stop really trying. You stop caring and stop asking questions but that's the fastest way to downgrade your brain which is definitely something that you don't want. You need to continue asking questions and craving new information or your brain will just stop working.

Think about why things are happening or what's happening in a given situation. You can even use your imagination in these situations by thinking about people you don't know or situations you have no control over. If you see two people talking think about why they are being so loud and what they might be talking about.

You don't need to actually go up and ask the people questions to find out the true answers. All you need to do is think about them in your own mind. Thinking about questions and answering them for yourself (even if you make up the answers) keeps your brain going and it keeps you focused on the things that are going on around you.

When you watch TV try to figure out what's happening at every moment. A good way to do it is by watching a movie you've never seen before that uses plot twists throughout. You'll be trying to figure out what's going to happen next by asking questions all the way through then you can see if you were right at the end.

CHAPTER 27- MAKE IT IMPORTANT

If you really want to make yourself smarter and your brain stronger then make it important. If you don't think that improving your brain is important than your brain won't either and remember what we said earlier about how the things you think become the things that are. You won't become stronger unless you work at it so be willing to make some changes.

If you want your brain to be stronger and smarter you need to make changes throughout your entire life and you need to keep those changes going for the rest of your life. You can't change your diet for a week and then expect your brain to stay stronger because it simply won't happen. You want to make sure that you're making changes you're willing to stick to.

Think about the activities you engage in as well. All of the ones we've talked about will help you but only if you really give them a chance and add them into your life continuously. That doesn't mean you have to do every single one of them every single day. You could decide that you're going to do a couple every day and a couple once a week or once a month. You may even decide that some of the activities just plain don't work for you in which case you can avoid those altogether. You won't learn much from something you don't like.

Keep track of the activities that work for you and how they work. That way you'll be able to increase those and avoid the ones that simply aren't helping and are only taking up your time.

Chapter 28- Change the Look

Getting bored with things the way they are? Get out and do something different in a totally different place. Human beings want to be safe and secure but they also want to take on change and adventure. You'll get bored being in the same place all the time and doing the same things.

As you fall into a rut and a routine your brain starts to get bored, stagnant and tired. You stop doing a lot of things simply because you're tired which is just because your brain isn't getting anything new. So give it something new, give it a change of scenery.

Travel is one of those things that people with money take for granted and those without often long for. It's something that your body actually craves as well because your body and brain crave change. Travelers can be some of the happiest people in the entire world because they've been able to experience new things constantly and avoid falling into a rut that stagnates their brain.

You don't need to move to another country or even go away for a long period of time to reap the benefits of travel. Even just a few weeks or a few days if that's all you have can make a huge difference and the change of scenery doesn't need to be far as long as it's different. Be willing to try new things and definitely be open to new experiences that will test your limits.

Find some way to fund a trip away from your hometown. Whatever amount of money you have will be plenty to do something fun whether it's only a few hours from home or all the way around the world. You need a vacation at least once a year that will help you escape from your humdrum life but how do you decide where to go?

1. Where have you always wanted to go from the time you were a child even if you've already been there before?

2. What types of landmarks are in your area or around the world that you have always wanted to go visit? Why do you want to visit them?

3. What is your favorite thing to do? If you like music then find a city that is famous for music, if you like ballet then find a place you can see a ballet, etc.

4. Where in the entire world do you think you would find the most relaxing and fun?

ABOUT THE AUTHOR

Hello, my name is Bowe Chaim Packer and I like to see myself as an open, *"wear my heart out on my sleeve"* kind of guy.

Some of the most important things to me in my life are:

- Laughing
- Kissing
- Holding hands
- Being playful
- Smiling
- Talking deeply with others
- Being loved
- Loving others
- Changing the world one person at a time (if my presence in your life doesn't make a difference then why am I here?) Hmmmmm, maybe that is a topic for another book. ;-)
- Learning from others (although often times I first resist). However, don't give up on me....
- Sharing ideas (no matter what they might be)
- Learning about others via most forms of contact.
- Traveling – hello, of course – almost forgot one of my favorite pass times.

Remember, LIFE is a journey for each and every one of us. We must never forget the things that are important to us or lose sight of what makes us happy.

Printed in Great Britain
by Amazon